Jubilant Whispers

An Anthology Of Poetry

by Michael H. Hanson

Published by
Diminuendo Press
Imprint of Cyberwizard Productions
1205 N. Saginaw Boulevard #D
PMB 224
Saginaw, Texas 76179

Jubilant Whispers
Copyright © 2010 Cyberwizard Productions

Individual poems copyright © 2010 Michael H. Hanson
ISBN: 978-1-936021-09-3

Library of Congress Control Number: 2009930024

Cover art by Helen Harrison

First Edition:

All rights reserved. No part of this publication may be reproduced or transmitted in any form or by any means, electronic or mechanical, including photocopying, recording, or any information storage and retrieval system, without the prior written permission of the publisher and the individual author, excepting brief quotes used in connection with reviews.

Dedication

for

Helen, Keith, Wayne, and Cynthia

my Sisters and Brothers

Acknowledgements

No man is an island, entire of itself. – John Donne

    Fond gratitude goes out to: my aunt and uncle Norma and Carl Brock, two gentle souls and voices of support throughout my life; sister-in-law Terry Hanson for taking the author photo; good friends Cedric and Joanette Egeli for rallying my poetic ambitions throughout the decade; Syracuse University comrades-in-arms Robert "Razz" Rasberry and Ralph Coviello for their fellowship across the years; online buddies Christopher Chaplin, Lynda Foley, Antonio Cervantes, Cairol Dawson, Lee Ann Kuruganti, Chris Bartholomew, Arthur Sanchez, Roena Vega, and Jaime Halbert for being nine enthusiastic wellsprings of goodwill; Massena Central High School English Teachers, Thomas Maxcy, Josephine MacKenzie, and Sandra Long for their active encouragement of my nascent teen writing skills; S.U. Newhouse Professors, Dr. Stanley Alten, Dr. Sharon Hollenback, and Prof. Richard L. Bryer for teaching me that the pursuit of excellence must be tempered with professionalism, discipline, and focus; co-worker Margie Rafferty for once again lending her excellent proofreading skills; all of my fellow poets at Zoetrope.com for their enthusiasm and support; and finally, all of my relatives; in-laws; friends; present and former coworkers; colleagues; and eclectic Internet pen pals whose emotional support, shared confidences, humor, feedback, insight, and stark but honest critiques have given me the courage to make this humble dream a reality.

From the depth of my heart, I thank you all.
Michael H. Hanson
Piscataway, NJ
Fall 2009

Table of Contents

Jubilant Whispers 1
A Song 2
Haunted 3
Naked in Waves 4
On Errant Days 5
Fire 6
The Poet Store 9
Conqueror Kiss 10
Annie 11
When I Was Small 12
Solitary Spring 15
Harbor Deck 16
First Kiss 18
Numb 19
Fading 22
I Dreamed 23
Family 25
Chance Met in Maryland 26
Summer's End 28
When My Brother Was Psychic 29
Forward 32
I Wanted 33
I Guess 35

This Maryland 36
Is It? 39
Candy Girl 40
Lifeline 41
Spring Blossoms 42
Lifesong 43
A Meal 44
Dreams and Fates 45
Gehenna Dreams 46
First Tryst 47
In The Trees 48
Brother's Child 4
A Lover's Tale 50
Autumn's Kiss 52
Valentine 53
Fragmenting 54
Goodbye 55
If I 56
Awaken 57
Cryptically Hip 58
On A Golden Shore 59
Wood Mosaic 61
What She Sees 62
First Love 63
In Sleep 64

Does Anybody 65
Strangers With Names 66
August Breathes 67
Pen Pals 68
Unrequited 69
Adrift 70
Homunculus 71
Walls 72
This Wintertide 73
King Midas's Brother 74
Genesis 75
Shadow Puppets 76
An Evening Shore 77
The Bread of Her Smile 78
No Longer 79
I Remember Her Kiss 80
Perhaps One Day 81
The Phelpsian Age 82
Repairman 83
Within My Heart 84
Cartoon Hitman 85
Supercollider 86
A Poem 87

Introduction

My second book of poetry. Wow. How could such a thing come to pass? I find myself momentarily nonplussed at this unexpected milestone in my life. Not quite two years ago (though it feels like yesterday) I put the final touches on a collection of sixty poems (fifty-nine rhyming and one free verse) that comprise the limited print run, hardcover edition titled *Autumn Blush*. It didn't exactly jump off the shelves. Yes, this is an old story in the world of literature, and one that I humbly embrace as part and parcel of the journey all writers find themselves on. Still, I had my doubts in late 2008 that I would ever get another such batch of my hopes, dreams, fears, and epiphanies into print again.

Not that I was short on material with which to fill a second collection! On the contrary, by the end of 2008 I found myself near the culmination of an unusual and ultimately uplifting six-month adventure at the writer-supportive website of Zoetrope.com. Created by famed film director Francis Ford Coppola, this website is a nexus for writers of all disciplines (poets, short story writers, novelists, playwrights, scriptwriters, you name it) and offers up the free opportunity to workshop one's written work amidst large groups of like-minded creative minds from all over the world. Upon discovering this wonderful place, I quickly found myself embracing the challenge and opportunity that such an entity offered. A fire was lit inside me, and I fanned the flames.

In the course of just half of a calendar year I wrote, from scratch, seventy-five poems that I threw out in the ring to do battle with harsh criticism, insightful reviews, and quite often, good advice. Some days I was jumping with joy, on others, punching the walls with frustration. I found myself re-conceiving, rewriting, and polishing my work to an extent I had never experienced before, and I believe I am a better poet for it. I certainly hope that the work contained in this anthology is proof of that. I leave it to you, the reader, to make that judgment. Roughly forty poems from that creative flood have found their way into this book. I am very proud of them.

So what separates "Jubilant Whispers" from my first collection of poems? What, if anything, marks it as a separate, breathing, living, entity in its own right and not just a sequel to "Autumn Blush?"

This time around, I decided to take chances. I decided to expand my output to embrace free verse as much as I did the loose, technically sloppy rhyming verse that had comprised the majority of my last collection. I decided to examine some of the more painful and emotionally traumatic moments in my childhood; events that I only recently realized had left deep scars in my psyche. I have looked back upon the length and breadth of my life to date (I'm in my 40's) and tried to give it some kind of insightful perspective, in poetry form. I impetuously wrote a tribute to one of the most famous love poems ever penned by an English-speaking poet. Heck, I even wrote a Villanelle and a Rondelet, as well as a couple of nineteenth century American sonnets, daring myself to remain within the tight constraints of such maddening forms.

On a whim, I submitted this hastily thrown together manuscript to Diminuendo Press mere months ago. The rest has been a whirlwind. Embrace your dreams.

With fondest regards,
Michael H. Hanson

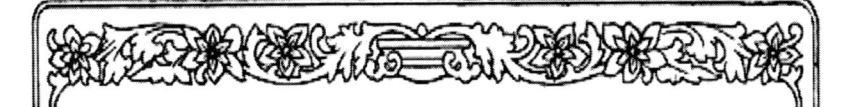

Jubilant Whispers

In my childhood I hid, shaking, behind
my mother's skirts, petrified by the world,
a cowering soul, a cowardly mole,
safe and secure deep inside of myself.

In my teenage years I bloomed awkwardly
stripping off coats of content baby fat
unnerved by the appeal of the fair sex
and desperate to shed my father's chains.

In my twenties I embraced the college
scene, the vibrant classes, the joy of beer,
that sweet thrill of guerilla filmmaking,
and the paradise, and crush, of first love.

In my thirties I took to married life,
a five day work week, buying a house,
doing yard work, small talk with my neighbors,
watching it decay to fated divorce.

Now in my forties I am cocooning
myself in poetry spun daily on
my computer screen, humble confessions,
lasting desires, and flickers of dim hope.

I feel a pressure building inside me,
an explosion of jubilant whispers.

A Song

Your eyes are the notes of a song,
born of finely lilting meter, and precision,
and rhythmic perfection.

Your laughter, silver, the words of a song,
joyous lyric, and script,
chiseled into polished eternity.

Your smile is the unity of a song,
made harmony, and melody,
in lush full lullaby.

Your heart.
Your wonderful vibrant glowing heart,
is an orchestra and choir
made whole upon
the unmatched opus of your glorious beauty.

And I play you, and sing you,
sweet draught of ecstasy
upon the strings of my soul
and the keys of my spirit
in awed enraptured unfettered adoration.

One perfect chord,
of resonant,
and undying,
LOVE.

Haunted

I'm haunted by my failing dreams
and all my petty fantasies
of fateful journeys, loves, and deeds
which cower like lost refugees.

I'm haunted by ambition's plea
to pen a noble righteous tale;
to write my generation's creed --
a flawless tome left un-assailed.

I'm haunted by my smitten heart
whose walls were breached with errant ease
by sweet infatuation's dart
and dark obsession's mortal need.

I'm haunted by my cowardice
which hides behind my every wish;
and ghosts of all my earthly dreads
now taunt and fester in my bed.

Naked in Waves

At ease, I walk into his studio
to greet a friend I made one bygone year.
Before his palette and his canvas lies
this vision, aesthetically austere.

She floats upon a graceful green divan.
Unfashionably long and lissom hair
that spills across her breasts to slowly pool
over endless limb, neck, and hip laid bare

where poise so coy defies embarrassment;
marble visage -- in studied quiet style,
thus makes this creature's exotic features,
and darkest charms a most bewitching guile.

Enthroned, barely tolerating her slaves,
on jade majestic sea, naked in waves.

On Errant Days

On errant days she whispers pleas
and prays for fortune's sweet bequest
yet hears, just silence, on her knees
and loneliness within her breast.

On errant days she dreams of knights
most dashing, resolute, and brave
who storm the castle of her frights
and mounted spirit her away.

On errant days she ponders fate
and all the wonders she's denied
and curses history's estate
whose promises are gilded lies.

She is the soul of womankind
with sufferings, sadly sublime.
One errant day her lot will shine
and on that day I'll make her mine.

Fire

This really happened.

While walking outside not too long ago I smelled a rancid pungent odor, the burning scent of something synthetic. And my nose wrinkled and I coughed and soon enough it wafted away from me. But for some reason I could not shake it. And so this strange unsettling shadow followed me into the deepest sleep of all.

And so I dreamed, but a dream, unlike any other. For in this dream I traveled back, far back. Into my past. My forgotten past. The archive of my soul. Back to when I was a boy.

A time I no longer knew. Back to when I was an Army brat. One of five. And my father was a Sergeant in the military. And we lived in the Perlacher Forest Army Housing Project in Munich, Germany.

It was 1968. And it was late in the year. And winter was on its way. And I was not a very bright child, at nearly seven years of age, for I was repeating the first grade. And we lived in a three-bedroom two-bathroom apartment on the third floor of a three-floor building. On-base housing.

And for the past week I had been writing to Santa Claus. Sharing the Sears and Roebuck catalog with my siblings. Filling letters with lists of toys that I wanted for Christmas.

GI Joe dolls, with many outfits, and accessories. And all manner of air-rifles, and toy machine guns, and cap pistols, that I could use when playing "Army," outside, with my brothers, filling the surrounding neighborhood with our savage yells of "You're dead!" and "I killed you!" and "No you didn't!"

And in school the spirit of the holidays was everywhere and our homeroom teacher taught us to cut paper angels and create elaborate snowflakes with a single sheet of paper and make our own greeting cards to show our parents. And though my birthday was still a week and a half away I kept reminding my mother that she had to make the cupcakes, the 30 chocolate cupcakes I would bring to my homeroom, on my seventh birthday, just like several of my classmates had already done this year.

And then, on a cold cloudy day this mid-December we had all come dressed in our good clothes to school for today we had our little Christmas celebration and we all sat behind our desks with smiles on our faces and our teacher, Ms. Mueller, handed out white candles to all. And then she lit all the candles that stood upon the center of our desks. And then she closed the blinds and turned out the lights. And then we all started singing "Silent Night, Holy Night." And it was like a sweet shroud of magic had settled upon us.

And then there was a piercing squeal. And the horror started. And there was a flash of yellow light to my right, brighter than all the candles combined. And there was a weird "whooshing" sound.

And a warm burst of air hit my right side. And a horrid awful chemical smell filled my nostrils in the semi-darkness. And then the overhead lights suddenly came on. And Ms. Mueller flew across the front of the room, a green army blanket in her arms. And she thrust the blanket upon my classmate Susan, whose head of thick fluffy brown curls had turned into a flaming torch and she was screaming, and burning, and writhing in the smoking remains of the diaphanous light-blue princess dress she had worn to school that day.

And then I awoke, in a dramatic Hollywood pool of sweat, and realizing this was not a dream. And I shivered, and knew, remembering, the truth of it. That I had managed to hide from for almost four decades, accosting me now, unforgivably, in middle age. That awful smell. That rancid nauseating unholy smell...

This really happened.

The Poet Store

Each morning I enter the poet store
to shop for fresh and crispy metaphors,
learned breads to feed my hungry readers,
and stockpiles of appropriate meter.

I nod and smile to my fellow shoppers
sly crafty misers hoarding their coppers
frugal consumers of forced brevity
frowning in judgment of my spending spree.

At the checkout counter my goods are bagged;
adverbs, adjectives, and stanzas that lag,
bottles of whimsy, large cans of free verse,
freeze-dried neuroses and muses that curse.

Squiring these groceries back to my home,
I dream of preparing a sumptuous poem.

Conqueror Kiss

(she said)

You have captured my heart, fine sir, with your smile
thus cast from within your dalliance, most unaware
as you stride across my vision's stage
alight, and bright, and most debonair.

You have snared my soul, dear man, and joyous rogue
with errant wisps of cast-off manly charms upon the winds
as your rich cerulean eyes shine
above your sweet captivating grin.

You have woven dreams, my Love, in your tapestry
and lyrics sown upon my dark fertile loneliness
blessing me with nocturnal wishes
and conquering me with but a kiss.

Annie

I still remember Annie's eyes
that shined so very poignantly
amidst soft pale and tender sighs
and warm impassioned dallying.

I still remember Annie's smile
whose timid welcoming allure
could tame a heart unduly wild
with gifts both radiant and pure.

I still remember Annie's kiss
thus granted on the midnight hour
a draught of sweet heavenly bliss
an intertwined angelic bower.

Her beauty haunts my memory
until the dawn awakens me.
And so, we end, this shadowed tryst
of mortal man and Will o' Wisp.

When I Was Small

I remember when I was small, the first time I took our dog Rusty, a full-grown reddish-brown purebred German Dachshund (that we kids had found abandoned in the neighborhood one night), on a walk, on a metal linked leash, outside of our apartment building in the Perlacher Forest Army Housing Project in Munich, Germany. Then Rusty heard another dog in the distance, and barked, and struggled against me to chase after it, and won, pulling the leash out of my weak little hands. And my eldest siblings went out and found him. And I was not allowed to walk him again.

I remember when I was small, my older brothers would go "comic trading." They would take a small cardboard box, filled with 50 or so odd comic books, DC, Marvel, you name it, all non-sequential, and walk from door to door in all of the apartment buildings that housed military families. They would knock on each door and then say "comic trade!" And if said family had a child who owned comics, they would sit down inside on the doorway, or in the hallway, haggling over comic trades, like professional baseball card entrepreneurs. But I could not do this myself, as the box was too heavy for me to carry for more than a few feet on my own.

I remember when I was small, I went on a picnic with my eldest sister, her boyfriend, and one of my school friends. And we sat beneath the large statue of "The Mustang," the stone horse, that, along with the statue of the elephant, was one of the two mascots of the Munich American High School. And the three of them climbed up onto the back of the massive granite horse. And they encouraged me to climb up also. But each time that I would rise up more than a foot off the ground, fear would hit me, and I shied back down, bitter, and ashamed, because it was impossibly tall and much too foreboding for me to ever conquer.

I remember when I was small, it was Christmas day. And both of my brothers and I received traditional German wood sleds (circa 1920's style) from Santa Claus. And there had been a thick snow fall the previous day. And my brothers threw on their coats, and mufflers, and mittens, and snowmobile boots, and I yelled that I wanted to go with them. And when we got outside I saw them slip their arms behind the bowed front skids of the sleds, slinging them on like backpacks. As they walked, the lower part of the sled would bounce several inches above the back of their knees. But when I tried to do this I was so short that the bottom of the sled kept bouncing against my Achilles tendons, and hurt me, and so I slowed them down, having so much trouble keeping up, complaining, whining all the way to Hospital Hill.

I remember when I was small, I spotted my two brothers get into a fight with a kid several years older (and several inches taller) than them. A bully. In moments my two fearless siblings wrestled him on the ground. I rushed to join the melee but couldn't figure out what to do. A couple of times I threw myself upon the large barbarians kicking leg. But then he would thrash it about, striking my head, or cheek, or arm, with his sneaker. And I would back off, crying, until I saw that no one was paying any attention to me and I quickly forgot my pains and jumped back in. I bit the giant twice on his big calf muscles, through his blue jeans, and that elicited wonderful glorious yelps of pain. And so this intruder eventually yelled out "uncle!" And my brothers granted their prisoner his furlough and we walked back home for supper, victors, all the while my brothers telling me, in intense and confidential voices, "don't tell anybody we got into a fight or Dad'll kill us! You got that Mike?"

Solitary Spring

Alone, in Spring, when Winter dies
and one is wont to ponder life
and contemplate the changing sky
and mother earth's three months of strife.

Apart, in Spring, when snowy melt
will slake the thirst of waking plants
and fading white reveals the welts
of Autumn bruises on the land.

Forlorn, in Spring, when you're alone
and breaking bread for just one mouth
and silence echoes in your home
as joyous birds depart the south.

And on this chill of early Spring
a rain of sorrows claw and cling.

Harbor Deck

A summer day.
Noon.
Standing on that beach house deck.
The inner harbor.
Audience to resting sailboats,
swimmers, and dog walkers.

Talking. Laughing.
Newly introduced.
You speak of art,
show me turpentine, and painter's knife,
how artists make their will apparent
upon small square canvases.

Your presence glows,
your smile a beacon,
introducing me to shadow, and light,
how one sees the world in its truest colors.
You spin magic with palette, and brush, defining
intent,
delicate strokes of bright multi-hued oils.

I fall, helpless, into the gentle rhythms of your sweet
voice.
Tides rise. Skin bakes.
Seagulls scream. Afternoon wanes.
Our once-clean hands freckle in rainbow pigments,
and SUPPER is finally yelled.
You leave to wash up.

My one and only art lesson
reaches its lonely end.

First Kiss

I sit and contemplate my life
a haunting archeology
and scavenge through a tomb most rife
with distant buried memories.

I feel my very mind now drift
unto the farthest shores of time
where I received a precious gift
replying in most fervent kind.

The awkwardness of flesh on flesh
exotic tangs and secret tastes
a pounding deep within my chest
the joy of youth's aggressive haste.

I dream of that enduring bliss
that sweet and magical first kiss.

Numb

It was my third day of Kindergarten in the school at the Perlacher Forest Army Housing Project in Munich, Germany and I still found everything so very confusing and my teacher was unhappy with me because I did not know how to tie my own shoelaces and I could tell that my crayon drawings were bad because I scribbled all over the coloring book pages when everyone else carefully filled in the picture outlines.

And days earlier, I was just too young to understand the conversations of my parents about my age and whether or not 4 years and 8 months was too young for me to start school and my mother saying she needed the break for half a day as raising five kids, me the fourth of five, was overwhelming and so every morning she would stand by the curb with me and see me board the bus that would take me to school.

And each day after school, the bus would pull up beside the long three-story apartment building that I called home and I would run to the right front door, and dash up the three flights of stairs in the main stairwell and reach for the knob of the door with the seven lacquered wood name plates each one displaying the name of a member of my family in fire-branded letters, in both English and Taiwanese (we had lived near an American Army base in Taiwan a few years earlier).

And so my third day of Kindergarten came to an end and I rode the school bus back to my home and it came to a stop in my neighborhood and I stepped off the bus onto the curb and I ran to the right front door of the nearest apartment building and I flew up the stairwell, to the third floor but this time something was wrong. The wood name-plates were not there.

And then the panic started, and I found that the door was locked. And I kicked and pounded on it and yelled "mommy!" But nothing happened. And so I ran back down the stairs. And outside. And up to the curb. And then all around myself. And I moved in a slow circle. And I saw how there were several of the large apartment buildings, which all looked exactly the same, all holding twelve apartments each, six to a stairwell. And each building had a code number on its side, and I could not remember ours.

And then I ran up the right stairwell of another building, and then another and the terror bubbled up in me, filling my stomach, and then my throat, and tears streamed down my eyes and made it difficult for me to see, and on every door where I arrived there were no wood name plates.

Finally, shattered, I found my way back to the curb where I had been dropped off and then I heard a terrible wailing voice, full of terror, and I realized it was my own voice, building with horror, screaming, one word, over and over again.

"Mommmmmyyyyyyyyy!"

And then an eternity passed, or maybe no time at all. And her arms were around me, and my red wet face smashed into her side. And she walked me to the correct apartment building, hugging me close speaking her soothing words, and sighs, and coos, those wonderful secret sounds that only a mother knows, and she sat me down on the living room couch, mute, beneath a blanket, because I shivered so. And that fear, that horrible terror that had drowned me, was now far away, and soon the shaking subsided. And I ignored my food during supper.

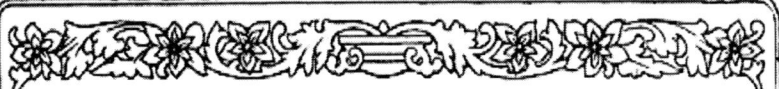

I didn't notice anyone around me that night. I did not hear the voices of my two brothers and my two sisters. And even my father's usual cutting baritone went unfelt, like water striking a rock.

And thus I fell into myself. A long spiraling endless drop. Down. Deep beneath the protection and safety of nothingness. A glorious wonderful absence of all.

Numb.

Fading

I raise a crass ceramic stein
and toast the sleeper in my soul
who dreams of quaffing passion's wine
and Autumn trysts and woodland strolls.

Impersonal this cycled bite
this endless Sisyphusian chore
this senseless repetitious rite
this empty daily hollow horror.

My spirit rails against my ribs
demanding promised sustenance
so long denied beneath the fib
of future raise and providence.

Each day a weaker shallow breath
this bane of incremental death.

I Dreamed

I dreamed I died last night
but not in some fantastic way
like pushed from a skyscraper's heights
and gunned down in a parking lot
nor screaming in a falling plane
crushed in a car on my cell phone
bleeding on a battlefield
or choking on a chicken bone.

Within my dream I woke upon
the very bed I know so well
yet different in the strangest way
that I sat up in sluggish fright
and startled that I felt so weak
I croaked a strange and fearful cry
then stumbled through my bathroom door
to face two aged bloodshot eyes.

And in the mirror of my dreams
my dead Father stared back at me
but unlike horrid memory
he looked now gaunt and world weary
until I saw his eyes were blue
when past were always hazel green
and so I came to see this truth
that I was frail and elderly.

I panicked through my rooms, amazed
to see the change of many years
dark peeling paint upon the walls

and flaking rugs on splintered floors
dull paintings crowding every space
old photos framed on dusty shelves
and yet no sign I shared this home
with any but my very self.

Exhaustion struck me deep within
and staggering I found my bed
whose ancient springs protested me
reclining with a shallow breath
I felt my will escaping me
and closing burning tear filled eyes
accepted my own deepest fear
that old and all alone I'd die.

And then I woke yet once again
not elderly but middle-aged
and ran to look upon my face
to see blonde hair instead of white
gaunt cheeks replaced with healthy fat
and all my teeth where they should be
and eyes still filled with dull delight
a quarter century reprieve.

Now one day later here I cower
upon the portal of that dream
and shamelessly I pray and plead
and ask the darkness what it brings.
Will I arise that aged man
so filled with dread and loneliness
or granted magic amnesty
awake both loved and bounteous?

Family

Thus born on near and distant shores
in regimented ranks were raised
five troopers from a time of yore
five warriors of weary gaze.

We forded Ancient Taiwan streams
and burned in Arizona's heat
and stormed Germanic castle greaves
'til our mad Sergeant met defeat.

With two red shaggy refugees
we braved a cold and northern home
and grew until we took our leave
of hearth for safe nomadic roads.

Maternal tolls, Paternal wounds,
retreating souls, outflanking doom.

Chance Met in Maryland

Thus was I invited to an evening party
deep in the Maryland wood
held within the main house built of sturdy oak walls
which rose to tall yet humble ceilings.
The living room of the home
of a celebrated master artist.

Wine and spirits flowed freely,
and my ears were flooded
with the iridescent language of art;
and smiles like floating candlelight
flickered about me,
and I wandered, nodded, and laughed.

While crossing this ocean of flesh,
I met the current of her dark eyes--
and in a moment was held fast,
anchored by my failing will to that corner of the room
beside a humble fireplace
whose glow was no less enchanting.

And so, I swayed to her beauty's wake--
the calm harbor of her smile,
cascading chestnut hair,
a dream of form and movement.
I struggled for stability and direction,
a flimsy raft to her wiles and charms.

Then the moment broke;
I once again stood within the still center--
so strangely calm,
and quiet,
and alone.

Summer's End

At summer's end, he bows his head
accepting nature's finite song,
and all those joys no longer fed
now wake to dark and hungry dawns.

At summer's end, she breathes a sigh
releasing all her fading dreams
of midnight walks 'neath moonlit skies
and passion's sensuality.

At summer's end, they share a kiss –
a most profound and sad embrace –
which marks the tragic death of bliss
and birth of autumn's haunting grace.

And so it is that hearts may mend
a crippling wound at summer's end.

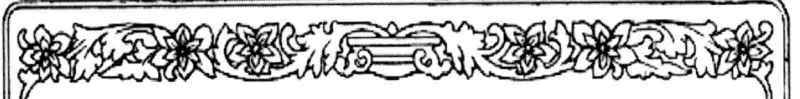

When My Brother Was Psychic

There was a time, long ago, when my brother was psychic.

He was ten years old. One of five American army brats, living in Perlacher Forest Army Housing in Munich, Germany. It was 1969. And our Father kept looking at Wayne intensely, strangely, every night during supper over the past week. Wayne laughed when Dad did this because he thought our Father was trying to be funny.

And then over the next few days Wayne overheard Dad make cryptic comments to our Mother in that resonating baritone of his.

"I think he heard me Martita. You see how he reacts? He says what is on the back of the cards! He guessed three face cards in a row! I tell you he's got the ability."

And then one weekend, on a Saturday morning without notice Dad told Wayne that the two of them were going to McGraw Kaserne, the Army Headquarters building in Munich. Wayne smiled! And left behind the jealous stares of his siblings.

And McGraw Kaserne was the coolest place. And they stepped into the neatest elevators ever, because there were no doors on them. And signs that warned you to stay behind yellow lines on the ground whenever the elevator was in motion.

And then my Father walked Wayne into a small office and up to a pleasant looking younger man dressed just like Dad. And they started talking.

"Yah, Rod?"

"Bill, I'd like to introduce you to my son. Wayne, this is Sergeant Bill Francke."

And then my Father looked at Wayne expectantly with his green hazel eyes that were the same color as Wayne's.

"Tell me. What is Sergeant Francke thinking?"

Wayne lost his breath.

"It's okay Wayne. You can do it. Tell Sergeant Francke what he is thinking."

Wayne just stared at both of them in shock. Not understanding. Not getting it. Scared.

"Well, uh, it's interesting to meet you young man. If you'll excuse me Rod I have an appointment."

And the Sergeant walked away, shaking his head.

And then our Father sighed in disappointment. And took my brother to the McGraw Kaserne Servomat! The vending machine room! The coolest room in the building!

Because it had "dozens" of vending machines made of shiny glistening glass and stainless steel which sold every single kind of food and drink imaginable. Sandwiches.

Hot soup. All many of candy bars. Fresh fruit. Peanuts. Soda pop. Water. Coffee. Tea.

Pizza. You name it. A modern high-tech cornucopia wondrous to behold. It was like some place out of the Jetsons, or Star Trek. And Dad bought Wayne an ice cream sandwich.

And then the two of them went back downstairs in the big elevators that had no doors and got inside our family's dull blue VW bug, and Dad turned to Wayne, and said in that pleasant baritone voice of his, "Now don't tell anyone about what happened this morning Wayne. If anyone asks, I just had to pick up some paperwork. Okay?"

And Wayne nodded his head, licking the remains of the delicious ice cream off of his lips.

And Wayne never spoke of this incident for the next

twenty-five years, until the day after our Father's funeral.

And so that, dear reader, is what really happened on the other side of the Atlantic Ocean, in that long ago time, when my brother was psychic.

Forward

I ponder that which I have lost
across the depth and span of time
as all my limitations pause
examining this dread decline.

The frankness of a morning run
the ease of gait, and stride, and sprint
the joy of burning heart and lung
the pride of hard exertion spent.

I walk on this macabre machine
no longer spry and blithely lithe
and chase pathetic hopes and dreams
to capture youth's enduring jibe.

I blunder on and rally rage
defiant in my mortal cage.

I Wanted

I wanted to be like Kwai Chang Kane, a Master of Kung Fu, traveling barefoot across the American old west, immune to the elements, at peace with the world, stomping Caucasian rednecks into the dirt with artistic moves of my hands and feet, using Crane Style and Tiger and Dragon, but always acting humble, right, I can't forget that...

I wanted to be like Robin the Boy Wonder and have a really cool legal guardian who was rich and I was his ward and we would have a secret identities and ride around in a rad black car and together, and we would rumble with bad guys and punch out their lights and we would wear really neat masks and capes...

I wanted to be like INS Reporter Karl Kolchak, The Night Stalker, tracking down weird creatures and monsters and strange things in the night and always defeat them with my wits, or better yet, through sheer dumb luck...

I wanted to be like Spock the Vulcan science officer on the Starship Enterprise, taller than the Captain, always laid back, unaffected by hurtful emotions with an extra long life span, three times as strong as a human with super hearing and an enlarged neo-cortex which gave me superior analytical abilities...

I wanted to be like Steve Austin, The Bionic Man, a former Astronaut barely alive who got bionic replacements for his right arm, right eye, and both legs, and I would be stronger than anyone else and leap the highest fences and run as fast as a speeding car though, I could only accomplish such feats in slow motion...

I wanted all of these things.

But then I grew up, and all that I got, was me.

I Guess

I guess I am a lonely soul
so disconnected from the world
my sad and weathered blue portals
are blind to every tempting pearl.

I guess I am a sorry sight
misshapen in both heart and mind
all bent within from petty blights
that spring from fiddling shameful crimes.

I guess I am a bitter fool
aware of my offensive flaws
each one a horrid uncut jewel
whose imperfections gnash and gnaw.

Pale veins invade my golden crown
and treasured flesh so slowly fades.
Despair has left my spirit bound --
imprisoned in this royal cave.

This Maryland

It is within the trees of Maryland
where all of my dreams become one.
Where endless trails lead on and on
and grassy slopes beckon unto me
where farmer and hunter share the land
and horse and cattle graze as friends
and early bird and morning dew
greet each day from their green dens.

It is in the soul of Maryland
where all of my hopes become one.
And sunlight blankets forest scape
and walls of oak and solid stone
carve their voices 'pon the Earth
in sweet songs of life, and existence
made whole beyond the distant banks
of waters darkly ebullient.

It is in the heart of Maryland
where all of my humanity becomes one.
And visiting, I reenter the world
upon a hillside, a warm farmhouse
and landscape tamed by loving hands
this home to gloried artisans
whose shadows grace a strong abode
two humble souls born of this land.

It is in the fields of Maryland
where human strife and soil became one
in conquered hill and rock and stump

and battles with thick summer air
the planting of precious life-bound seeds
of corn, soybean, wheat, and barley
and raising beasts upon such feed
cattle, sheep, and poultry.

It is in the streets of Maryland
where bustle and leisure become one
where brick and cobblestone unite
and thoroughfares and sidewalk paths
all lead down to a harbor scene
where business, travel, trade are done
the mortar of community
a wise inspired union.

It is in the rains of Maryland
where water and life become one
where river, lake, and stream delight
where beaver dams grow adamant
and rain gardens flank the urban forts
and sailboats flirt just off the shore
and swimming folk play water games
and fish and frog and snake endure.

It is in the memory of Maryland
where truth and history become one
and time gives up its mysteries
and facts surrender all their secrets
birthplace of Tubman, Douglass, Brent
the brave defense of Antietam
the doom of Edgar Allen Poe
the hunt for Lincoln's Assassin.

It is in the bosom of Maryland
where faith and religion become one
and fellowship and brotherhood
run hand in hand with sisterhood
and strong beliefs breed stronger hopes
and worship beds with noble pride
and joyful prayer resonates
and all of God and man combine.

It is in the beauty of Maryland
where loneliness and desire become one
and I stumble 'pon a woodland nymph
whose aching tender loveliness
and gorgeous saddened dark fey eyes
blind me to all sanity
and to this very day I sing
her graceful form so willowy.

And it is in the whole of Maryland
that I have come full circle
and travel back unto myself
and arrive at my own beginning
and my hubris has been extinguished
and I fall 'pon hands and knees and weep
at last accepting the haunting kiss
of nature's sweet embracing sleep.

This ancient hallowed hinterland
this loving home, this Maryland.

Is it?

Is it too late to rise anew
and dare to face a brilliant dawn
and breathe in all the world's sweet blooms
and free my heart from all its bonds?

Is it too late to tender bliss
upon a damsel I hold dear
and feed her lips a gentle kiss
and wash away her every tear?

Is it too late to have a life
and all the hopes that wishes bring
and stride in pride through daily strife
and smile, and laugh, and love, and sing?

This urgent plea, I shout, on high
beneath a dark unfeeling sky.

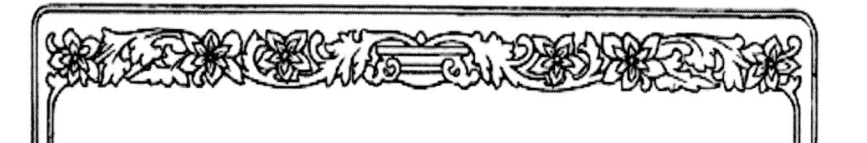

Candy Girl

i work beside this confectionary dish
a petite sweet, with eyes like licorice

her smile makes this little boy say yum
her breath the rum of bubble gum

but it ain't funny, my bit-o-honey
i crave like Goodtime's chocolate bunnies

this neat carbohydrate treat stays wrapped
withholding her unfolding
from this cold vanilla Frap

so I give Jack Daniels' lollypops the licks
and drink hot shots of peppermint schnapps
and Godiva-spiked chocolate Nestles Quik

candy's dandy
liquor's quicker

Lifeline

I read your words, my longtime friend
which gently flow across my screen
and promise that my heart will mend
and once again fulfill its need.

I read your words, which tender hope
and echo from your humble lips
the strength of your kind safety rope
and comfort of your comradeship.

I read your words, from far away
this letter from a distant shore
this priceless gift which never fades
when passing through my rural door.

And as your spirit fills my gaze
it whispers dreams of brighter days.

Spring Blossoms

    I would take your hand on this warm Spring day, and lead you through a field of soft downy grasses. Smiling, I offer soothing sips from a carafe of golden dandelion wine. And joyously we run and shout at white-freckled cerulean skies, until finally we collapse, laughing, at the foot of the flowering Sakura tree.

    I do not know who you are, and you probably don't know me, but I sense your spirit, out there, adrift, like mine, floating on the cool yet tender breeze that makes these white and pink cherry blossoms shiver, seductively, on their long delicate branches.

Lifesong

I breathe a great expanse of air
and fill my lungs with fervent strength
and grace death's challenge with a dare
to test my life throughout it's length.

I feed upon the luscious fruit
long born of bent and learned trees
whose wisdom are the hoary roots
of all of man's absurdities.

I love beneath a silver moon
the object of my fierce desire
engendering a wondrous swoon
which culminates in mortal fire.

My soul is graced with livid runes
a map of all my journey's wounds.

A Meal

I prepare a meal, for you, my darling,
(with humble hands washed in a mountain stream)
in my simple solitary kitchen;
the warming expectation of a dream.

I knead bread dough with slow gentle squeezes;
cut vegetables with an ancient knife;
crush rosemary and grind black pepper;
spritz olive oil until the fish is right.

I anoint my modest table with clean,
fraying linen, candles of yellow bee's wax;
a plate of cold and salty Amish butter;
decanted wine in an etched crystal flask.

I tie back white floral-patterned curtains;
raise the shades and open up the blinds --
and an auburn sunbeam blesses this meal;
most redolent in lavender and chive.

I wait for you on the front porch wiping
hot virgin crumbs on blue-jeaned thighs.
I bask in quiet anticipation
of one perfect tranquil moment in time.

Dreams and Fates

In the one hand are all my dreams,
the other, fates.
From sleeping lands that I have seen
I choose the joy of blessed dreams.
Though pondering the world of late,
I feel the pull of waking life
whose noble cause engenders fates
to battle strife
and war on hate.

My soul is wedded to my dreams,
and heart to fates.
Rejecting all life's agonies
my spirit favors lovely dreams.
But then my heart feels evil's mate,
whose loathesome wretched horrid bite
so stirs the hunger of my fates
I prey on spite
and ravage hate.

And so I bid farewell to dreams,
and greet my fates.
Though sleeping realms are quite serene
we are not meant for lotus dreams.
There is a world we can create
with humble hands and renewed sight,
endowing paths to all our fates
with gentle light
that splinters hate.

Gehenna Dreams

Slipp'ry and slimy and slith'ring
creeping and cravenly crawling
dripping and dragging and drooling
wickedly wilting and with'ring.

Scaly and scabby and screaming
hairy and hoary and hissing
cystic and cackling corrupting
stalking and sticking and stabbing.

Flapping and flaking and fleeing
plundered and plunging and pleading
crying and cracking and cringing
wraithfully wrathfully wailing!

Thus dark Gehenna dreams, beneath.
The horrors of all human feats.

First Tryst

The fumbling awkwardness of sin
intoxicating radiance
the drive of hot adrenaline
the bane of inexperience.

The heat and spark of shared desire
igniting passion's very blood
a holocaust of sensual fire
a boiling unstoppable flood.

Insanity without control
this madness of eternity
an aftermath of mingled souls
adrift within infinity.

Beyond all rationality
life's dark and sweetest mystery.

In The Trees

God hear my voice within these scrawls
I pray that someone understands
I write my blood upon these walls
Petition of a hopeless man.

The treasure of my heart you see
She was my true and only love
And hand in hand she walked with me
Until Hell struck us from above.

No one believed my horrid claims
Too weirdly tragic without proof
When I awoke near her remains
The victim of scale, claw, and tooth.

Now soon they'll strap me to the chair
To blame for what is in the trees
"Avoid the park you must beware!"
I tear my throat with endless screams.

Brother's Child

I look upon my brother's child
and see the face of distant life
the echoed breath of ancient trials
inherited and sorrowed strife.

I see a trail of wandering
and desert caravans anon
I see existence prospering
always traveling on and on.

This child's endearing smile endures
one part of this unending dream
a song of wisdom true and pure
a hope passed through eternity.

This blessed unbroken memory
this testament to destiny.

A Lovers Tale

It is late in the month of November
when maple trees, sleeping, no longer bleed;
and my night hike grows sullen and sober;
my heart feels a chill mysterious need.

Thus I wrestle and fight with the mountain
so swift in reckless and savage ascent
that I soon find a warm breathing fountain
draining from crimson and soft pulsing vents.

Bathing my worries and cleansing my fears
at peace like a child afloat in the womb.
Calliope whispers, "I'll join you dear."
Specters of love 'neath a still sapphire moon.

Some time later my eyes spot a phantom --
a shadowed strange plot of earth newly raised;
and so stepping up out of the fountain
I walk mesmerized with unblinking gaze.

And thus shaking I see the gray marker;
trembling and deaf to Calliope's wails;
and I know as the moon becomes darker
that something's amiss, and beyond the pale.

So I read the harsh blackened inscription
which burrows down to the roots of my soul --
unjust prey of an awful affliction;
my shy love who left me three years ago.

And now gasping I wake feeling smothered.
Shaking and sweating I crawl from my bed
and I whimper and cry for my lover
this dream which my heart has unnaturally wed.

Thus for years I have dared my reflection
courage to journey this terrible way.
Now I sever life's tender affection
and guilt, and sorrow, and shame bleach away.

I will enter the realm of the mountain
to join Calliope's wandering soul;
and we'll swim and we'll live by the fountain
whose clear gentle waters eternally flow.

And my vision becomes ever clearer
and fiery demons stop clawing my chest;
and with her warm sweet lips drawing nearer
I know that my spirit can finally rest.

Autumn's Kiss

The breath of autumn welcomes me
with cool and lissome whispering
that falls among sweet, gentle leaves
and sets my lips to whistling.

We walk along a forest path
which winds around a lovely knoll –
a musky, pungent, floral bath,
a drink that purifies my soul.

She circles with bewitching grace
adorned in nature's gaudy dress
and offers up a gorgeous face
that pledges peaceful, charming rest.

Thus, I am granted my last wish,
embraced in autumn's luscious kiss.

Valentine

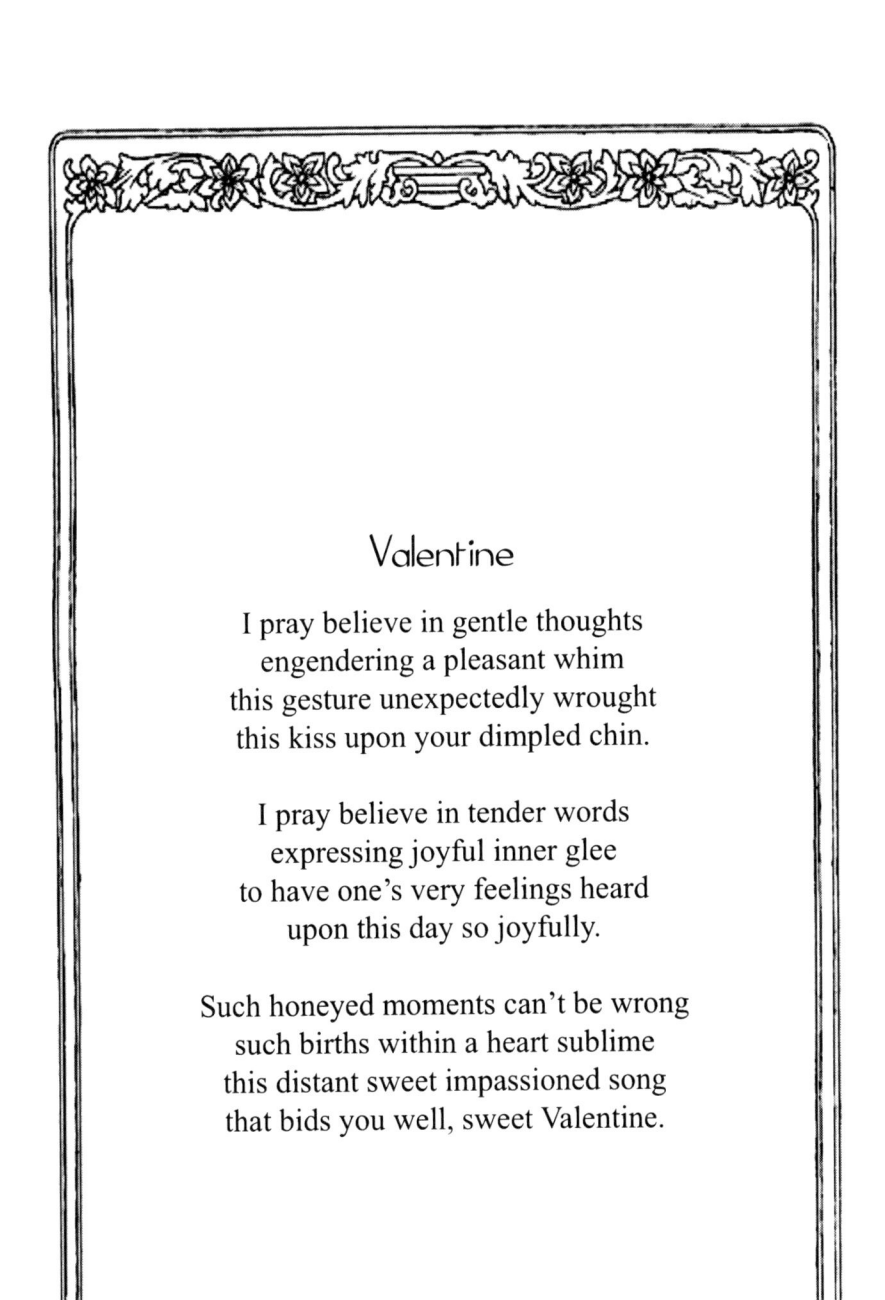

I pray believe in gentle thoughts
engendering a pleasant whim
this gesture unexpectedly wrought
this kiss upon your dimpled chin.

I pray believe in tender words
expressing joyful inner glee
to have one's very feelings heard
upon this day so joyfully.

Such honeyed moments can't be wrong
such births within a heart sublime
this distant sweet impassioned song
that bids you well, sweet Valentine.

Fragmenting

How ordinary, and how commonplace
these plain and miniscule covalent bonds
that shape reality, our existence;
make us solid, and singularly whole.

What comprises life's simple unsung glues?
Joy of parent and child, sweet cherished hugs;
loving spousal kisses, sibling laughter --
harmonic strings that twine the heart and soul.

And when these covenants disintegrate --
death, divorce, or simple relocation;
the matrix of human spirit unspools --
a slow chain-reaction of ruptured hope.

Thus, loneliness is made fissionable;
our very essence begins...fragmenting.

Goodbye

Goodbyes are often fragile jewels
too oft displaying nervous knees
which mark a moment strangely ruled
by formal quaint civility.

And in this strange and structured air
a most important hope is lost
that all our common dreams and cares
will be the proper mannered cost.

So take a care to ponder well
the balance that your life has run
and pray express your best farewell
so that it is a lasting one.

And do not leave here sad or grim
for change is life's most constant peer
and visions of our mutual whims
will comfort you in passing years.

If I

If I escaped these crippling walls
of haunting insecurity
would you accept my timid gall
and listen to my tender plea?

If I revealed my inner truth
bared helpless 'neath an Autumn sky
would you accept this humble proof
that my respect is not a lie?

If I approached you for awhile
no longer circling widdershins
would you accept my gentle smile
and trust me as your paladin?

My heart would sing triumphantly
if your sweet eyes but noticed me.

Awaken

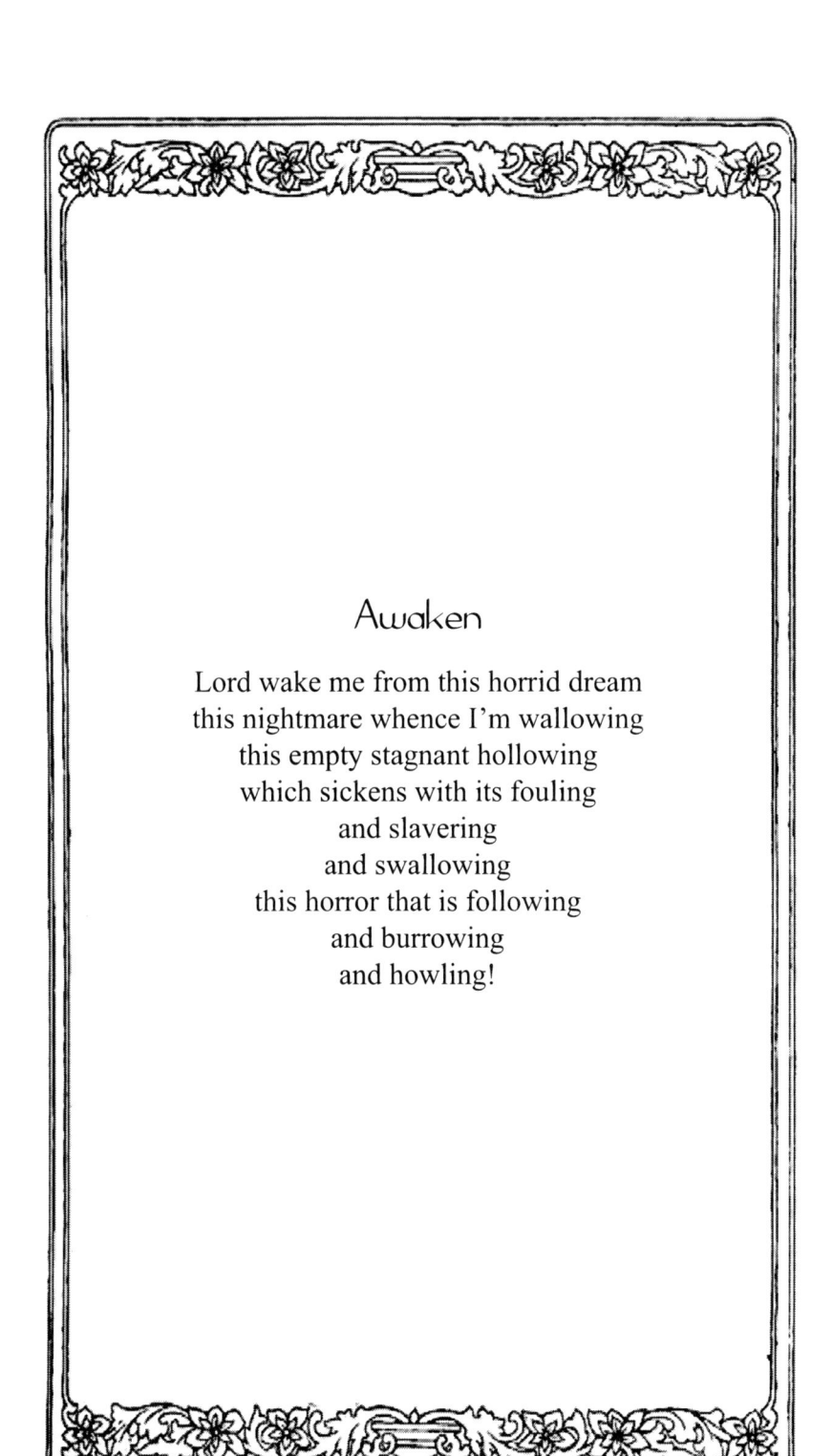

Lord wake me from this horrid dream
this nightmare whence I'm wallowing
this empty stagnant hollowing
which sickens with its fouling
and slavering
and swallowing
this horror that is following
and burrowing
and howling!

Cryptically Hip

She dances far outside my real --
amidst the shades of cooler trees;
ethereal with haught repeal;
beyond my grasp and lesser needs.

A charmed enigma in my dreams;
Bohemian in voice and thought.
a canvas rich with twilight creeds --
sweet southern siren I once sought.

Utopian in grace and form;
both fanciful and tightly sealed.
Her will a strangely hidden storm
unfettered by my pale appeals.

This weak confession from my lips --
this kitschy post-modern worship.
This chic and high-def cyber chip --
this goddess, cryptically hip.

On A Golden Shore*

SHE moves in Beauty, like the sea
of breathing green and azure tide,
this lovely mermaid from the deep
whose rolling tresses and soft eyes
go peaceful to that gentle glee
which majesty cannot deny.

On golden shores her ancient dance,
of muted move and precious pose,
enjoins in love and soul enhanced
anointed hands in sweet repose,
expressing moments burned in chance,
where all of form and rhythm flow.

'Pon haunted knee and sculptured thigh,
unspoken whispers genuflect,
in shades of passion still and shy,
serenity and soul reflect,
a silken neck and perfect line,
a purity of self respect.

Thus slowing wave, and inner light
and tears of oceanic grace
soon bathe in rivers far from sight
within her tender blushing face
'neath sun ablaze and blinding bright
revealing virtue true and chaste.

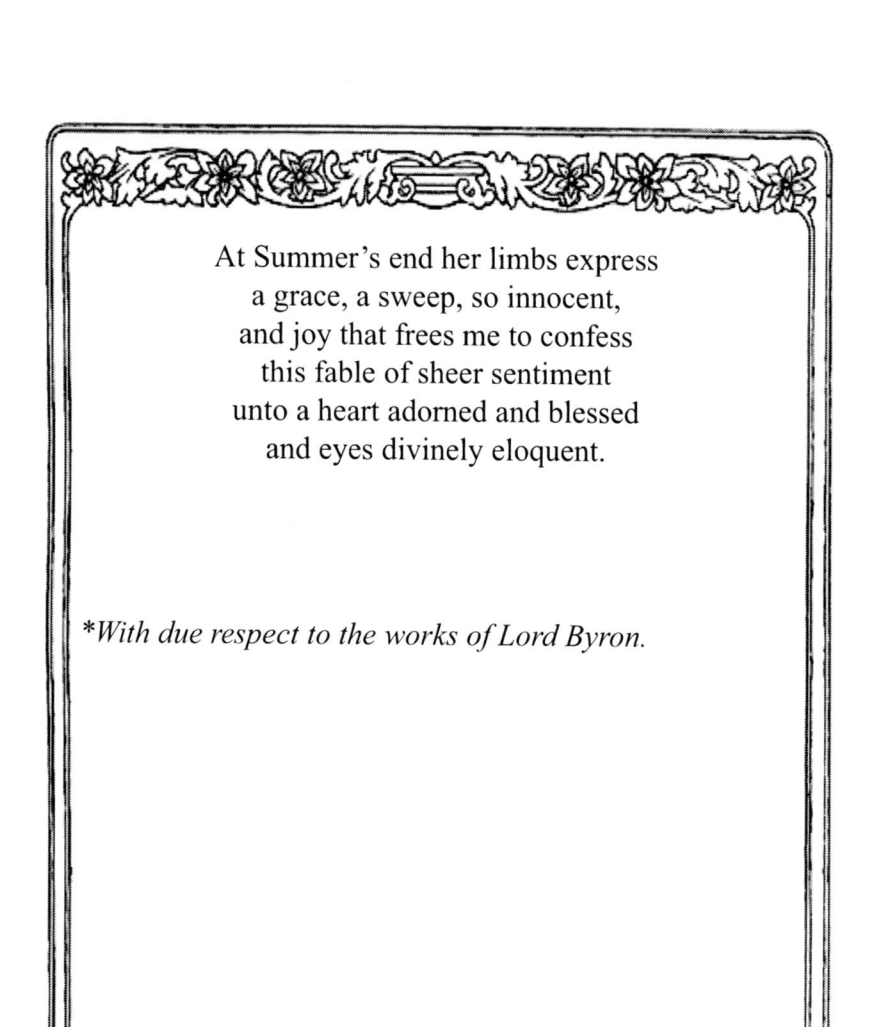

At Summer's end her limbs express
a grace, a sweep, so innocent,
and joy that frees me to confess
this fable of sheer sentiment
unto a heart adorned and blessed
and eyes divinely eloquent.

With due respect to the works of Lord Byron.

Wood Mosaic

It hangs on my far kitchen wall,
quaint, rustic family heirloom,
a blending of beautiful wood
and scene from a hard, simpler time.

The craftsmanship is quite subtle
this marriage of skill and folk art
created by my grandfather
within the autumn of his life.

I never knew him, cold old man --
granger, handyman, carpenter,
surly artisan in the rough.
Distant, simple North Country son.

I gaze upon his mosaic
birthed of tree trunk, chisel, and stain.
It haunts my soul, as Farmer and
horse-cart travel on, always on…

What She Sees

Beneath the stars she oft reflects
beside a gentle sleeping sea
with flowing hair 'pon silken neck
and all her dreams a mystery.

Well mirrored in her tender eyes
the grace of Heaven's majesty
this spectacle of jeweled sky
a wondrous cosmic symphony.

How glorious must be her thoughts
beyond this crude hyperbole
a treasure trove we all have sought
a realm of sheer serenity.

The radiance of what she sees.
Sweet moments in eternity.

First Love

And our entire world is born
made whole upon the very strength
of our attraction's every morn
that wakes in loving sweet embrace.

Twin torsos hot electric beat
'tween moments of eternal peace
in raptured joyous harmony
and cries of passion's fierce release.

Oh gloried stretch of Autumn days
inert to coming Winter's chill
most unaware of future pain
and blatant signs portending ill.

Three months, and then, this angel left
my ravaged heart, and soul, bereft.

In Sleep

In sleep, my troubles fade away
undressed in naked eloquence
where all my fears are led astray
and all my hopes grow radiant.

In sleep, I conquer every task
and stumble not while journeying
and no one sees beneath the mask
of my obsessive worrying.

In sleep, I'm granted every wish
and lack for neither friend nor love
and wallow in most selfish bliss
as sacred songs rain from above.

Through sweet eternity I roam
until I wake up all alone.

Does Anybody

Does anybody see my tears
which bleed from cuts of bitter grief
a horrid pulse of salty jeers
that scurry like dark fleeing thieves?

Does anybody hear my heart
a savage howling wounded beast
a demon nearly torn apart
in love's devouring selfish feast?

Does anybody feel my soul
that writhes within a raging fire
of burning lust and breathing coals
that houses all my fierce desires?

Unthinkable that none now know
my sufferings and hellish woes;
the spectacle of fiddling shames
that ravages inside my veins.

Strangers With Names

Strangers with names and civilized manners
we shared an afternoon of adventure,
not colleagues, but growing familiars
window shopping and sipping fruit smoothies.

We met through common humble circumstance
connecting by mutual dalliance
thus fate introduced me to your brown eyes
and I fell, entangled, within your spell.

Sweet auburn summer light fell on the day
while I watched you walking away, so poised,
so elegant with charming composure,
a precious dream reaching its waking end.

Weekend passed and I left that cape island
pining over the memory of you.
Now I write my passive aggressive poems
that slowly boldly whisper, I love you.

August Breathes

Fair August breathes a fiery laugh
and dimples on bright golden sands
a bawdy flirt across the map
sashaying through all summer lands.

The warmest smile throughout the year
a hug that welcomes one and all
most joyous kiss 'neath blue veneer
this heated tryst before the fall.

These final waves of amber love
(thus break upon a mortal shore)
whose total days count thirty one
and join those months of August yore.

Pen Pals

Across the waves of time we've talked
and shared our dreams and wants
reliving tales of life and love
adventures, journeys, jaunts.

And in your words I've seen a face
a gentle trusting girl
whose tender smiles and timid eyes
have set men's hearts awhirl.

And knowing that we're far away
a continent apart
I know that I am truly safe
from my own selfish heart.

For we are friends within our words
which bind us like a book
and gives us strength and honesty
against which Gods have shook.

And pondering eternity
and these few words I've sent
remember me in future days
and all my blandishments

Unrequited

To never love creates a curse
upon a nobley humbled home
whose silent beds remain averse
to raucously pedantic poems.

To never love predicts a crime
whose end is writ on prison walls
by wraiths who spend their Christmastime
exchanging looks down childless halls.

To never love makes bright the shame
of one whose dull and listless soul
would revel in a pauper's claim
that others' passions pay his toll.

In short, my heart is like a room
whose light may enter from above;
but curtains keep this room in gloom
of one whose heart may never love.

Adrift

I'm cut adrift, beyond my fears --
no longer tethered to this world
where all my bitter angry tears
lie strewn like lost forgotten pearls.

I'm cut adrift, thus freed of chains
no longer bound by petty creeds,
and all my life's enduring banes
now bleach and painlessly recede.

I'm cut adrift to roam alone,
no longer tied by sweet desire --
a skeleton of mundane bones
devoid of all erotic fire.

Adrift, I float from day to day
untouched, unhurt, and unafraid.

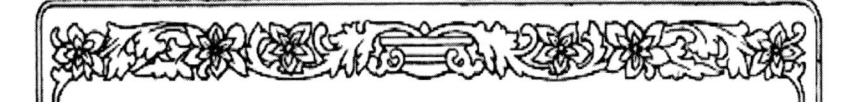

Homunculus

I walk through the crowded hallways of life
slightly out of step with humanity's
odd syncopated alien movement
and weirdly hypnotic exotic acts.

Sweet interaction of parent and child,
courtship protocols, impassioned lovers,
entitled rich screwing over the poor,
the horrors of physical violence.

I try to communicate my unease
with all of these strange complex rituals
but am halted by diamond barriers
of thick impenetrable terror.

And so I live in constant daily dread
that my performance will be uncovered
and my inner machinations exposed;
unmasking my fictitious existence.

Walls

I am surrounded by beauty:
delicate, small geometries;
gold and silver gilded-age frames --
portals to far exotic lands.

Pastel, charcoal, and oil pigments,
the epidermis of art --
these wonders of lush creation
mark the borders of my kingdom.

Magic seasons of sun, snow, leaves;
charming sirens forever posed.
They all withstand my loneliness.
I am surrounded by beauty.

This Wintertide

Angelic choirs of laughing rhyme
which giggling kids can't hold inside;
we smell the pitch of blushing pine
that snuggles us at wintertide.

Sweet crystal flakes upon our tongues,
flimsy toboggans all can ride.
We gulp hot cider like a sponge
and sculpture snow at wintertide.

The thrill of daily greeting cards,
warm crushing hugs at fireside,
most loving call beckons homeward
uniting us at wintertide.

Now one score years and nine have passed
since my last family yuletide.
I reminisce a distant past
that haunts me on this wintertide.

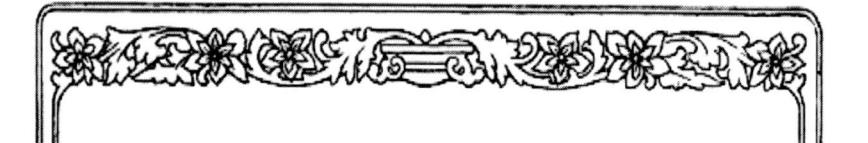

King Midas's Brother

I look in the mirror and see the change:
a transmutation of grand alchemy;
pearly rivulets streaming through my crown;
lustrous, noble, precious mineral veins.

My beard, once a bright alloy of amber
and auburn flax framing both cheek and chin,
now under siege by moonlit metalsmiths,
pale armies of ivory tinkerers.

Fundamental elemental weaver –
this deeper primal Dionysian spell
altering all that I touch to witness
my slow transformation, into silver.

Genesis

And so it found me
naked and wandering
through barren valleys of shame
no longer blind to the lies
and plasters of my existence
which taunted me as I stumbled
flailing, clawing desperately
for some greater truth, and hope,
but finding only dead answers
penned by silent ghosts.

Why now, deep in the middle
of this fractured journey
was this introduction made?
I do not know, but it sang
to me. Songs of roaring surf;
flaming mountain tops;
the grief of dying gods;
cyclopean forests of musky green
and love as deep and moving
as a summer's day or a winter's eve.

And we embraced, this passion and I;
a consummation of dream and craft,
a sea change,
this rupture in the void,
and most feral birth.

Shadow Puppets

You find me wandering, in search of love
across a landscape of shadow puppets
happily grafted to transitory
marionette strings of wealth/fame/beauty.

I try to touch one, but meet emptiness;
a hollow construct of breathless voices,
shallow paper plaything lacking substance,
oblivious to flesh and blood appeals.

So I pen my songs of simple whimsy
ignored by twilight wraiths with tin toy ears,
excelsior guts, icy dead doll eyes;
callous automatons of ambition.

I am alone on this silent playground.
Tell me, where do the other children go?

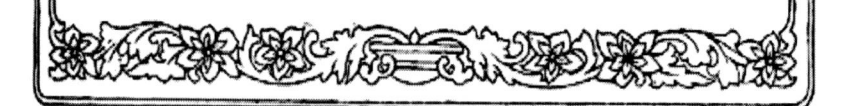

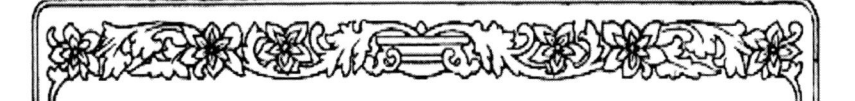

An Evening Shore

Would you wait upon an evening shore
anticipating that first sight of me
approaching like some prince from timeless yore --
aspect of brave, gentle nobility?

Would passion brace the patience of your heart
and grant me moments of eternity
to cross this harsh gap like some mythic dart,
collapsing breathless with forehead to knee?

Could you accept all my humble worship
and words of frank and tender sentiment
that bridge and join our dry and thirsty lips
beneath this dusk star's blushing sacrament?

Enjoined, entwined, and intermingling cries;
hammers in my heart, sweet fires in your eyes.

The Bread of Her Smile

Her very presence is a fine banquet,
she nourishes the emptiness in me,
joyous horns of plenty blossom from her,
truly she is the Goddess of Repast.

A harsh hunger cries out within my soul
a loneliness of weakness and despair.
My mouth waters in anticipation
of this pious, sensual eucharist.

Her haunting eyes are the spice of beauty,
I drink the wine of her honeyed laughter.
A pauper, I worship at her table
and I feast upon the bread of her smile.

No Longer

I no longer want to feed my critics
who denounce the truth of my humble gems;
deconstructors of flowery visions
condemning the pain that bleeds from my pen.

I no longer want to be an author
pursuing a fame and glorious prize
creating a bright immortal novel
worshipped by scholars both righteous and wise.

I no longer want to be a poet
who opens his veins and pumps out his life
in unwholesome displays of sorry rhyme,
bombastic grammar, and dramatic strife.

I no longer want to be a writer –
an insecure purveyor of letters –
glorified schemer and naked dreamer,
pretentiously proud, aping my betters.

I want to climb the highest of mountains,
shouting my rage in lightning and thunder,
shaking my fist in defiance of fate,
damning my crippling fortunes asunder.

I Remember Her Kiss

I remember her kiss
that glorious tickle
of rich soaking pressure
and flowery caress
with its smooth, warm sweetness
lightning dance between tongues
a giving and taking
a sharing and bonding
joined gentle surrender
a sighing, a dying,
and raw rampaging
wet moment,
peaceful bliss.
I remember her kiss.

Perhaps One Day

My longing for you continues to grow,
Unhampered by distance and passing time,
And perhaps one day I will tell you so.

On that morning we met, how could I know,
Your shy loveliness would curse me to pine?
My longing for you continues to grow.

Look now, and see, what your beauty has sown
A deeply rooted most passionate vine,
And mayhaps one day I will tell you so.

The absence of your smile should bring me low,
My memory drinks it, the sweetest wine.
My longing for you continues to grow.

My inner conviction wills me to show,
you a most humble, confessional sign,
And perchance one day I will tell you so.

But for now this cowardice is my foe
Unscalable mountain I wish to climb.
Thus all my longings continue to grow,
And I pray one day I can tell you so.

The Phelpsian Age

I watched a demigod perform tonight
competing in an ancient foreign land,
a man of most singular physical
attributes, and unnatural focus.

Athlete worship is so overrated
when measured against the social problems
of this day and age... then Mike dives like a
bolt of lightning into challenged waters

and like some otherworldly hybrid of
human flesh and aquatic juggernaut
this unrelenting missile of muscle
and bone wages maritime combat, and wins!

Unparalleled triumphant victor of
eight fiercely mythic Olympic battles.

Repairman

My father, an appliance repairman,
could mend the insides of things.
He could ferret out hidden flaws,
replace broken parts with working ones.

Looking within each washer, dryer,
refrigerator, each stove, instinctively
he knew the whole of them, how they
bind in mechanical harmony.

But for some unfathomable reason
this did not translate to flesh and bone--
the foundations of human spirit,
for HE was damaged, in need of repair.

Was it an unloved, repressive childhood,
or a North Korean cannon shell? Its
shrapnel slaying his platoon, his buddies,
blasting him into coma, slashing his optic nerve.

Amoral liar, sexual predator, cowardly sociopath--
was it a cracked bearing in the gears of your mind,
or a frayed belt upon the drum of your heart?
Repairman, why couldn't you fix your own
malfunctioning soul?

Within My Heart

Within my heart a secret hides
Far from the truth of questing eyes,
Encased in shadowed mystery,
A shy retiring refugee
Whose every single dream has died.

A prisoner of shame and pride,
Intelligent yet far from wise,
And on his bitter bed he dreams
Within my heart.

He knows the world exists outside,
A wondrous realm where lovers fly,
While troubadours sing joyously,
Despite those earthly agonies,
Crippling the spirit which resides
Within my heart.

Cartoon Hitman

Bugs Bunny failed my wabbit test
his wucky foot hangs on my chest.
And that star-belly Sneetch who snitched
I pitched headwess into a ditch.

Yes Daffy's wisp dwove me insane
I pushed that qwack out of a pwane.
And Popeye's stutter ticked me off
siwenced by my Kawishnikov.

He drawled too slow that southern hound
so I had huckleberry dwowned.
Magilla did not take the hint
his hands and feet sold for a mint.

When I'm awound all cartoons hide.
I pwactice animaticide.

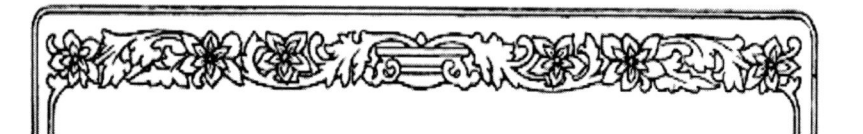

Supercollider

Each of us is a super collider,
a complex and gargantuan engine
arcanely generating torturous
accelerations of hurt and regret.

Feelings, wounds that move at the speed of thought
through labyrinthine tunnels in our souls;
sufferings that build fatal momentum,
circling to an inevitable crash.

But there are also particles of joy,
fragments of beauty, and atoms of trust;
the physics of mutual attraction,
when two hearts collide in a burst of love.

A Poem

Every one of us is a poem,
a soft fleshy composition
conveying rich, hidden meanings
and articulated beauty.

Every one of us is a verse,
a hymn writ on parchments of skin
that whispers the sweetest of dreams
and whimsies of laughter and tears.

Every one of us is a song,
a fierce, prosaic batch of years;
a fabled, mystic lullaby
dwelling in shadowed harmonies.

Every one of us is a dance,
a cry of rhythym and movement;
joyous gesture, raw expression.
A beginning, middle, and end.

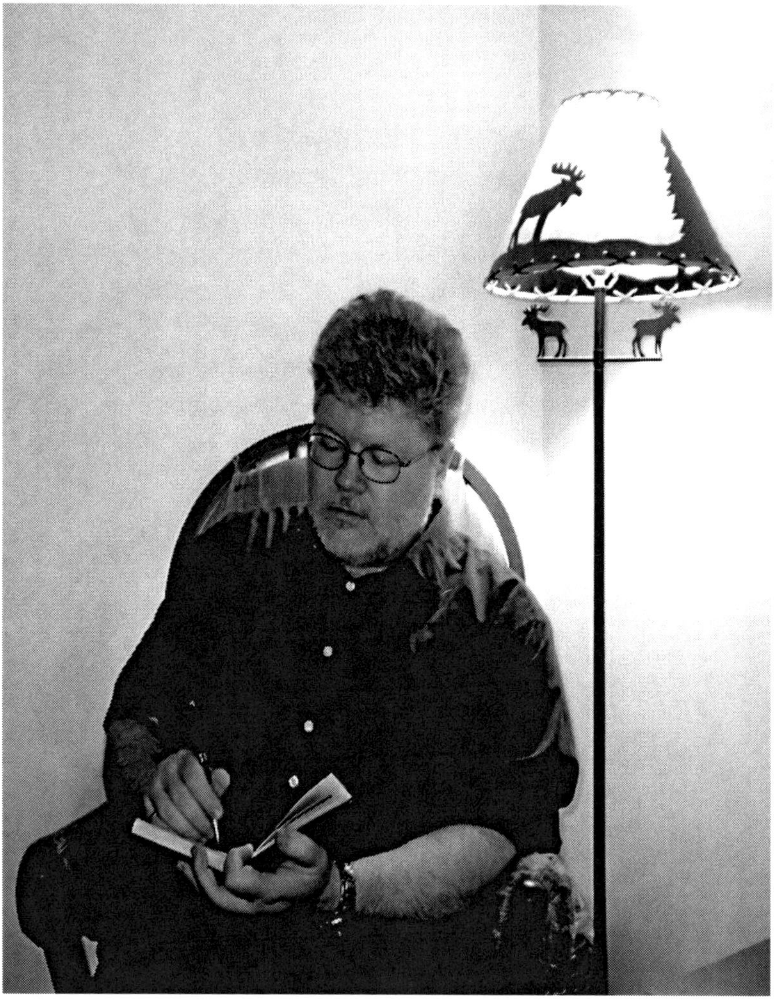

Michael H. Hanson, the son of a U.S. Army Sergeant and a Nurse, was born in Potsdam, NY, amidst the icy climes of New York State's Northcountry. He spent the first ten years of his life as an Army Brat, one of five, living in such disparate locales as: Taipei, Taiwan; Munich, Germany; Camp Drum, NY; and Fort Huachuca, AZ, before finally settling down in his mother's home town of Massena, NY. He began writing his first poems for the local newspaper at the age of 15. He graduated from Massena Central High School and spent a short stint in the U.S. Air Force. Michael went on to become a Film Production major at Syracuse University, and graduated with a Bachelor of Science degree from the Newhouse School of Public Communications in 1989.

Though he mostly dabbled in the writing of poems throughout the first two decades of his adult life, it was the convergence of three powerful events that finally opened his soul, and his heart, to the overwhelming passion of poetry. The sudden, unexpected death of his mother from pancreatic cancer, the difficult dissolution of a 12-year marriage, and a two week tour of Ireland (where he spread a portion of his mother's ashes on the west coast) lit a bonfire inside Michael, a creative conflagration that now burns intensely throughout his many evocative, beautiful, and haunting poems.

Michael's first collection of poetry "Autumn Blush" was published by YaYe Books in 2008. "Jubilant Whispers" is his second book of poetry. Michael currently lives in New Jersey where he spends his free time spinning introspective verse, and tales of the fantastic in his small but cosy garden apartment.

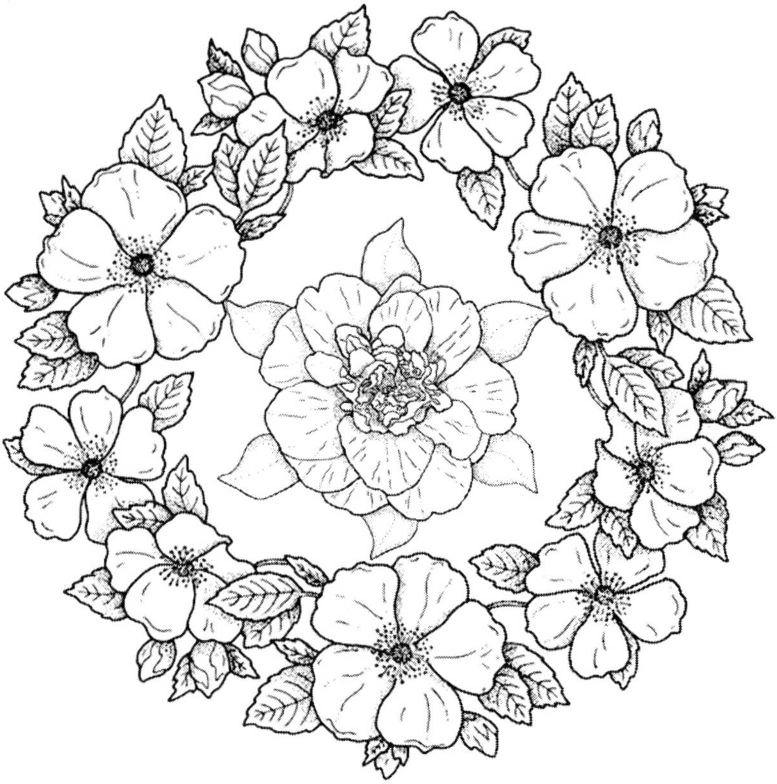

Breinigsville, PA USA
18 June 2010
240124BV00006B/25/P

9 781936 021093